An OWS Ink Anthology

Written By
AF Stewart
Anna Schoenbach
Dorothy Tinker
Ed Ahern
Janet McCann
JK Allen
Karla Linn Merrifield
Kerry EB Black
Ynes Malakova
Stacy Overby
Rebecca R Pierce
Matthew Wilson

Primal Elements

An OWS Ink Anthology

OWS Ink, LLC Press, United States

Copyright © 2018 by OWS Ink LLC

Cover: Rebekah Jonesy of OWS Ink

All rights reserved. Printed in the United States of America. No part of this book may be used or reproduced in any manner whatsoever without written permission except in the case of brief quotations embodied in critical articles or reviews.

For information contact:

OWS Ink, LLC 1603 Capitol Ave.Cheyenne, WY 82001 http://ourwriteside.com

ISBN ebook:

ISBN print:

First Edition: May 2018

Foreword

Our Write Side is Your Write Side too. We at Our Write Side are all about community, building and fostering support for authors and readers everywhere. Our Write Side has grown to include marketing and editing services, masterclasses, and our publishing arm, OWS Ink, LLC. We love every kind of writing, not just fiction, and are putting more focus on poetry inside of our community. So we are happy to announce that OWS Ink will publish a poetry anthology like this one every year, starting with Ambrosia which was released in 2017. This year the focus was on the elements; air, fire, water, earth, and spirit. These elements have connections to our thoughts, to our feelings, and to how we see ourselves in the world. And these primal forces have inspired our poets in vastly different ways. From wind-whipped storms to searing thoughts to murderous connections, come explore these vivid poems in Primal Elements today.

Air	1
Wind	3
Anemoi: Mercy Whisper	4
Chinook	6
Ascendant Wind	8
Wrath	9
I smoke a cigarette	11
The Storm Wind	13
TORNADO WARNING	14
Breath	15
Sparrow	17
Breadth of Life	19
Beaufort 7	20
Fire.	21
Fire	23
Helios: Devil's Flight	24
Inferno	26
Fire Bird	27
Gifts of Olympus	28
Slow Burn	30
I Subside	32
Immolation	34
Queen of Fire	36
SURFING	37
Phoenix	39
Firelight	41

Water	43
Water	45
Euphrosyne: First Snow	46
Black Mirror	48
Your Hands	49
Eisfeld	51
Off Silver Bank	53
The Moon and the Sea	55
Changeling	57
THE ORIGIN OF DREAMS	59
Ice Out	62
Veiled Water	63
Water Women	64
Mother Earth	67
Earth	69
Demeter: Hollow Earth	70
Beaufort 4: All the Elements	72
Crafted from Mountains	74
Stone Giant	76
Petrichor	79
THE CRONE'S ATRIUM	81
In the End	83
Moonlight	85
Progress	87
Under the Earth	89
Duels of Cursed Men	91

Spirit 93
Spirit 95
She Who Hears the Gods 96
Goodbye, Glowing Eyes....................99
Vixen 100
A Universe of Spirit 102
Author Bios.......................................104
Other Anthologies by Our Write Side
....128
Books by Our Write Side..................134

Air. From a lover's breath to the beating winds of a hurricane, air gives us life and can wreak havoc. This is known as the element of thoughts and intellect. Air is known to move and flex in much the same way as the poems in this section. From the tickle of dancing grass blades to the electrical current of a storm in the air, follow along with the flow of these poems.

Wind

Kerry E.B. Black

She sighed his name with airy breath

And dreamed he'd call her wife,

Unaware when she shared the news

Her dearest friend felt strife.

A triangle within his heart

Left secrets undisclosed.

Mandolin winds tore him apart

Untold love now exposed.

Anemoi: Mercy Whisper

Ynes Malakova

Into the cup I blow,

A ripple of Earl Grey

Hitting the paper rim

As my eyes cut across the conference room,

Meeting my colleague's gaze.

My nerves rattle—

Loose shutters—

Against

His vortex of jargon.

All eyes are on me.

The air is thick with silence,

Fear stifling the breath in my throat.

I do not know,

I do not know

The answer

But must respond,

Regardless.

The air conditioner lurches overhead,
A light stream of air
Tickling my skin
Through the weave of my suit jacket.
I hear you in its thrum—
Benevolence—
Smiling at my ignorance,
Sharing your song:

"All eyes are mortal,
Unknowing—
Unseeing—"
Absent of the secret that
I do not know.

So I inhale,
Slow and deep,
Straighten my gaze,
And push a breath through my lips.

Chinook

Stacy Overby

Feathers brush across reddened skin.

A susurration ripples through grass-
-
then nothing.

Waiting.

Heart beats.

Feathers become claws that whip and grab.

The grass howls and crumples

thrashed and battered.

Energy running wild,

blasting all without discernment.

No end in sight.

Waiting.

Heart beats.

Claws fade to feathers against chapped skin.

Screams thin to whispers

through broken stalks once more.

Ascendant Wind
A. F. Stewart

On wing they fly, the black birds,

swooping ravens dancing through air

past clouds and currents and wind

Scattered in gusts and gale

dark dots along the storm

On wing they fly, the black birds

See their inky feathers flutter

in breeze, past the swaying trees

swooping ravens dancing through air

On nature's breath, they ascend

extended wings scaling the tempest

past clouds and currents and wind

Wrath

Anna Schoenbach

What will you do when the storm hits?

Your friend is in the way of the blast –

It is a sudden gust.

And though only curtains of stray rain lash you,

They are struck with all of the thunder and fury

of an angered Poseidon.

The sky, once clear, has darkened to a sinister green.

The waves, once calm, have whipped into a frenzy.

What do you do? Would you save her?

No -- You would freeze,

As if your flowing blood had become ice –

Solid, unmoving, and cold.

Nothing, you would do nothing.

Dazed by the storm as it passes,

As the sky clears to a pale white,

Over the flotsam and the jetsam,

You are left in the wreckage of its wake.

I smoke a cigarette

JK Allen

I smoke a cigarette
sucking in air through my teeth
the wind whips my hair behind me
a rushing sound in my ear

The air is all around me
though I cannot see it
it smells of mint and ashes
(cool as spring rain at night)
as it brushes against my skin
trailing goosebumps

I exhale
watching the smoke billow out from me
like a dragon's plume
never ending, the steam
puffs and morphs into a cloud

soft wisps that dissipate into the sky

I cannot see the air,
but it is there
enveloping me in sheets of wind
and I think of you
existing without my sight
standing in a night like this
sharing someone else's smile
I close my eyes
take one last hit
and exhale

The Storm Wind
Ed Ahern

gusts and surges
like an unchained guard dog,
strewing dust and pollen,
flashing the naked underside
of leaves,
and tossing meadow grass
like ruffled bear fur,
spinning from side to side
in drunken dance,
a rioting brawl that cannot last,
and ends
with a watery flourish of thunder.

TORNADO WARNING

Janet McCann

cat and I curled
looking at dark sky
cut by black branches and lightning

the weather radio
repeating in its monotone
tornado warning, then its location

speaking in all caps
warning us to take cover
not to go out into the windy night

in the electric air
slight disturbance of
long summer sleep a slight fear

tingles arms and fur
inside, outside, hairs crackling
along power lines wake up wake up

Breath

Karla Linn Merrifield

I have come once again to the place

of our continent's abundant bromeliads—

to Florida—to live on warm air,

as those green creatures

of subtropical swamps do.

How little they require of the world.

Air plants some people call them,

others employ the elegant Greek epiphyte.

I would like to be one among them,

live a life receiving the beneficence

of bald cypress trees, asking only

for a fragile grasp, most delicate touch—

like warm air—of their skin.

May they be well-rooted hosts

and I a sprite-like guest, their human

bromeliad, Call me Ephiphyte.
I dream of air, warm air,
so little of this Earth.

Sparrow

Dorothy Tinker

I am the Sparrow who flits through the stalks.

Bamboo is my home and its whispers, my talk.

My flitters and shadow are all that you see.

Ignore you my true Self and claim it's not me.

You threaten my Self, my bamboo you will take.

With swords and with tongues, my true soul you will rake.

But lone I am not before you, the unkind.

The shadow of sparrows is not all you'll find.

You cannot see Dragon, curled up, breathing smoke.

Tiger awaits you and champs at the yoke.

Know not you Phoenix, whose beauty shines through.

Forges her pathways, to Self, she stays true.

And you ignore Vixen, whose wisdom is rare.

See you her beauty; her mind, give no care.

How Ursa Mother evades your true sight!

Towers, protective, won't run from a fight.

Together we build up in bamboo so strong.

Something you'd keep from us all for so long.

So take down my forest; I dare you, no less.

Let the world see us, our strength, a fortress.

I am the Sparrow, but I am not weak.

Friends I rely on, and they too on me.

Breadth of Life

Rebecca R. Pierce

The breath of life never breathed easily.

Its first utterance was a cry of pain.

Expelled from one world and to the next

Its slick path marked by a red stain.

Its second gasp was a beggar's call.

Ghostly fingers with their beseeching clasp

Alms for the lonely and disheartened,

A soul that seeks itself to grasp.

From exhalation to exaltation,

The weight of a life is measure in words.

One storm ends in a wheezing sigh,

While a gentle breeze is flying birds.

Beaufort 7

Karla Linn Merrifield

Wind

invades

white clouds,

the magpie's wings.

Taos Mountain gusts

are deep exhalations

of a local prophet gone

sage-mad in her high, dry desert.

She makes more than aspens
quake— she takes

me like a leaf to the valley of self.

Fire. From the reborn Phoenix to burning thoughts setting our mind ablaze, fire is the element of passion. It offers comforting heat or roaring pain without prejudice, proving that fire represents both extremes. But just like that Phoenix transforming anew, this element carries with it the hope leaving pain in the ashes. The following poems explore the lick and sear of the dancing flames.

Fire
Kerry E.B. Black

Burning bright as the guiding star
Upon an autumn night
A fever wracked his erstwhile soul
Consumed every delight
With passion overpowering
He then exerted might
Allowed wrongful rage to consume
His grasp of wrong and right.

Helios: Devil's Flight
Ynes Malakova

Fingers trembling,
The engine sputters
And turns over, finally,
The needle pointing to red.
I'm on fumes—
Fuel and hope
Flashed to vapor.

Charred rubber smolders
And gravel whips from my tail:
Shards of a fractured life.
I shriek down Willow Lane
Rousing sleeping infants
And elderly men,
Sleepy eyes meeting a
White demon
Igniting 2 AM porches.

Help me,
Please—

Stop me,
Please—

The words fizzle;
Effluvium—
Exhaust—
They choke my victims.

I pray that
Salvation
Is around the curb,
Just one more street
To set ablaze.

Inferno

Anna Schoenbach

I am an inferno.

My skin crackles in the heat of my ideas.

Ideas so brilliant they burn,

so intense they consume everything.

I writhe – they are too much, too fast, and all ablaze.

Not for long.

Mere moments, and they are but flickering embers and ash.

Wisps of regret, drifting through my fingers,

leaving me naked and shivering in the emptiness.

Fire Bird
A. F. Stewart

From the ashes blaze and burn
razed in immolation renaissance
Soar, my Phoenix, in glorious cremation

A thousand cracks scorched,
into hope splintered existence
from the ashes blaze and burn

Finale circled to new beginning
outside the fire cleansed purity
razed in immolation renaissance

Light the sky in illustrious flames
Blistering a trail of mortality, a beacon
Soar, my Phoenix, in glorious cremation

Gifts of Olympus

Matthew Wilson

I have stolen the God's treasure
into that dark mountain I trespassed
to steal the fire that would save
mother from the coming winter.

The gods laugh as their children freeze
and I have seen them dance too long
in that light that basks their Olympus
toasting great feasts to their vanity.

Through the brightening hills I ran
sharing fire to banish the dark
freeing prisoners from their shadows
showing men were more than puppets.

Now the Gods have chained me here

on a rock none are permitted to near

except mom who has no fear of night

now her boy has given the world a sun

Slow Burn
Rebecca R. Pierce

I dance in orange veils for you.
In the quiet dark, my bones crack.
Red-hot veins run through my limbs,
Bearing light yet turning black.

I dream in flames my greener days,
When heavenward, my fingertips
Played a song for the wind.
The sun kissed me with golden lips
And shook birds loose from my hair.
Closing my eyes, I'm almost there.

A star-freckled sky, the dewy grass,
The wash of rain, the crunch of snow...
I trembled with youthful passion—
But that was a lifetime ago.

A deeper love, a slower burn
Whittles me down to ash and bone.
Fire flowers bloom from gnarled hands
A phoenix sings in its new home.
I was made for sharper mettle.
A house aglow and a warming kettle.

I Subside
JK Allen

I flame
orange light licking at my skin
brimstone heat searing
I am parched,
tongue cracked, ash white
as smoke crawls from my mouth
down to sooted black feet
reaching you with silent steps

I crackle,
pops and hisses punctuating
every rising noise
issuing from my raging teeth
snaps of sound that leap
from my lips to yours

But you are stony

impervious to scorch marks
marbled white
—a statue—
cold and impossibly distant.

I subside
the fire subdues
but becomes hotter at my core,
a burning coal in my chest
embers glowing
red eyes staring
stoked so they will never die

Immolation

Stacy Overby

In the cracking and the heat
all is lost and yet is found
in amongst the great deceit.

Snapping. Popping. Such a sound.
Crunching. Hissing. Burning bright.
Blackness spreading all around.

Golden shades—a wondrous sight!
Shining waves will now ensnare,
climbing high'r into the night.

Sulfur smell filling the air,
calling this from in my mind.
On it goes without a care.

Heat will grow ever unkind,

never give them a reprieve—
all who seek will end up blind.

Ne'er again will they deceive—
truth now burns for all to see.
I will force them to believe.

Cross me not, it's my decree,
for I give no mercy here.
Those who do will learn to flee.

Shadows are what most men fear,
not the brightness drawing near.

Queen of Fire
Matthew Wilson

I was born in the pit of fire
mother's last surviving daughter
since my sisters died in her war
against the king of moonlit water.

To save her empire she decided
to abandon warfare and her pride
to hand me to the water's son
to live there as his lawful bride.

Our making is not of happy endings
if we touch then one would die
fire and water do not mix
never touching under the sky.

I was born in the pit of fire
mother's madness is in me
now I have killed this selfish queen
and I will have my victory.

SURFING
Janet McCann

I google my first friend,

Find only her obit, with her married name

But it is she, thin girl with wispy brown hair

Who took a dozen vitamins each day

In the fifth grade, telling me at lunch

What they all were. I google another

And get no trace, a third, another obit.

I guess I should post a personal: "Wanted:

Anyone who grew up in Chatham, New Jersey

In the forties. Purpose: to talk about

The underground fires at the edge of town,

How we all thought these were

Hell. How the smoke came up

In puffs from the crack and we
imagined

Corridors of flame and screaming
people.

The tyrant kindergarten teachers,

The library open two hours on
Tuesdays

And Thursdays on some lady's
second floor.

Please send a black-and-white

Photograph of who you were then.

We will drink iced tea from
aluminum

Glasses and remember."

Phoenix

Dorothy Tinker

I am the Phoenix, my soul burning bright.
Through arts and through passion, I live in my light.
I've not been a phoenix for all of my life.
I've been through the wringer, through pain and through strife.
I once was a queen, majestic and kind.
But then torn asunder, naught left but my mind.
In ashes they left me, my hope was no more.
No moxie, no purpose, 'twas cut to the core.
That wasn't the end, though, to Self I clung dear.
Cold spark in the ashes of hatred and fear.

Determined, I reached for all warmth I could find.

The flames I renewed as wings formed from my mind.

I dressed in old feathers, perfected with age.

They stirred up my soul song to break my ash cage.

I relit the death pyre, from flames I arose

and sang for the freedom of all hearts and souls.

So beat me or burn me or snuff out my flames,

I'll keep on renewing, untethered, unchained.

For I am the Phoenix, my song renews all.

I gather my flames, build them up, and stand tall.

Firelight

Ed Ahern

The allure of an open fire,
warmth aside,
is an inarticulate wish
for pyromancy,
for the flames to reveal
in flickers
the whys and wherefores
of living.
Thoughts swirl in updrafts,
grasping for
the random patterns,
tantalized
by closeness to ineffable
substance.

Water is life and surrounds us in abundance. Taking the shape of whatever contains it, it may seem a passive element. But water will cut rock, carving its own path through the stone because it is persistent. These poems speak of water's yin and yang qualities, exploring the hunting ground of sirens and winter storms. Come see what calm waters hide and the black waters reflect.

Water

Kerry E.B. Black

Her hair spread like golden seaweed
A halo round her head
He held her there beneath the lake
Until she ended dead.
He cradled her within his arms
And kissed her bloated lips
A ring he placed upon left hand
Then 'neath the silt she slips
Lungs filled with water in a grave
Without the passage fee
Charon felt pity for the girl
To Gaea made a plea.

Euphrosyne: First Snow

Ynes Malakova

The frost in the South is fleeting
Like a two-year-old's joy:
Footprints in fresh snow
Gone by noon.

Six years have passed
Since he left the Northwest:
Exchanged his scarves and
Parkas and tuques
For t-shirts and sandals.

So he walks past me quickly,
Barefoot,
Into the weatherman's winter fluke,
Strong, calloused feet meeting
The frozen patio slab,
A thin robe covering him
Just below the knees.

He will soon wake our son,

Hoist him on his back,

Whisk him into the backyard flurries,

Bathe his plump cheeks and red hair

In wet, sticky sky-kisses,

But in this moment

He stands alone,

Encased in a crystalline,

Transient solitude,

Soft at the edges

Already melting away—

I watch from the doorway

As he raises his arms,

Calling,

Through upturned palms:

Welcome sleet,

Welcome cold!

Welcome heavens,

Welcome home!

Black Mirror

Anna Schoenbach

Lake water glitters like black glass in a mirror.

The sky is a shadow upon the surface, not reflected.

Details are mimicked and warped by its motion.

Looking down, the water is not a mirror, not a window,

but a shroud: Hiding its secrets, magnifying its fears.

Water-weeds are snakes, fish are monsters, stones are fangs.

We do not see through the murk.

The paddle dips below, the paddle returns, the paddle shimmers.

Like black glass in a mirror.

The kayak glides – ever on the surface,

Free from the distortions beneath.

Your Hands

JK Allen

She has water hands

that line the curved edges of lakes

tips trailing

like ripples across my skin,

she holds my palm

in hers

white fingers

filled with waning moonlight,

and like water

she makes me buoyant

rising to the surface

kissed with cool lips

wet with morning dew.

I float in her smile

in her outstretched hands, deep as bruised shadows

that lift me

carrying me out with the tide

I ebb and flow around her

pulled towards her

sometimes tempestuous heart

and I am swallowed by

billowing waves

that break to reveal storm
strewn grey mornings

filled with golden light

sparking across the water.

But it's those hands that hold me

lifting, leading

through swells and calm seas
alike

and I live for those golden
mornings

glittering in her hands.

Eisfeld

Stacy Overby

In silence falling ever more,
a frigid peaceful blanket here.
It's growing thicker every hour
'til all is buried out of sight.

The wind has teeth that now bite deep
as hungry mouths are seeking heat.
They draw it out of living things
that venture out into this world.

Its needle fingers penetrate,
deposit hoar frost in their wake.
It stiffens limbs and fogs the mind
as crystals form beneath the skin

A vital thing so coats the world,

sustaining life in this harsh place.

But, lurking there a deathly chill

will claim the life that lingers there.

Off Silver Bank

Karla Linn Merrifield

The stars are our brothers,
the whales are our brothers,
you are my brothers.

Andromeda sings,
Megaptera novaeangliae sings,
the three of us sing these

starry paths by this inner compass,
drift of the ocean embraced
—immersed   amidst—

swimming with giants,
staring into a behemoth's eye,
looking deeply inside one another.

The greatest of hearts on our planet

beats in waves of recognition;

we will always return to the sea.

Three old souls on a boat are we

rocking in the love of leviathans, spouting

to highest bestudded heavens: O warm life!

The Moon and the Sea

Rebecca R. Pierce

The moon pulls me with the tide.

It washes cold silver o'er each rippling wave.

I fold and unfold myself but cannot hide.

The merciless light is a crippling lave,

And all my secrets thus will blanch

As each wave crashes in avalanche.

Do not stir me tonight

Because I am water and you are stone.

And all your wiles are maddening bright

When I want to be alone.

Rushing and hushing, in love and hate,

All through the night, I vacillate!

And I dash myself against the rocks,

I splash myself against the shore.

Still the beaming smile mocks

Making me quake and reach for more.

The more I sigh, the more I heave…

As darkness and light interweave.

When at last I am but spent,

And my crumpled soul is smooth and still.

Then, at last, will you relent

And make your kisses soothe, tranquil?

Thus are we locked in intimacy,

For you are the moon, and I am the sea.

Changeling

Dorothy Tinker

I am the Changeling, my form is not firm.

I spend my days listening, observing to learn.

At times I'm a dragon, my breath fire hot.

My wingspan's a marvel, in air I'm besot.

At others, a panther, my steps whisper soft.

The trees are my homeland, I hunt from aloft.

Then there's my candor, naiveté grand.

I know you, I see you, I can understand.

But angel gets broken, and devil comes out.

I'll curse you, I'll damn you, take joy in my shouts.

Then come the siblings, they're twins, you might say.

Boy I am, girl I am, change day to day.

Like water I alter, from this me to that.

From demon to angel, from dragon to cat.

Don't let me deceive you, I do hold beliefs.

They come out in whispers, and sighs of relief.

Now you may believe that I'm one just like you.

Be careful, I'm shifting, won't show you what's true.

Yet too from myself, I have hidden away.

My truth I'm discovering as night turns to day.

I am the Changeling, my true Self's a team.

Frozen I am now, but ice turns to steam.

THE ORIGIN OF DREAMS

Janet McCann

I'm in the office loo, ready to leave the booth

when I see there is water on the floor

and an alligator sticks his head under the door.

I scream, jump up,

stand on the toilet and scream and scream,

and an eight-foot-tall man in a uniform

grabs me, tucks me under his arm

and sets me down in the hall.

I breathe relief, but look—

baby alligators slipping under the door,

water oozing. I kick them away

and they bounce off the walls like rubber

but they start to grow, slither toward me

and I climb up to a high window ledge

and sit there hoping the giant will come back

and pluck me safe, while through the window

I see everyone running, fleeing the campus.

*

J. told me how it was at their house

when Harvey came, the dark waters

rolling down the street, they running

upstairs with food, drink, anything they could

grab, and then they were rescued by boat,

each clutching a dog. When she tells me

of the panic, the wild rush, dark waters

rise in my mind.

On the ledge I watch the alligators

snap at my feet. The campus is empty now,

the rain is falling.

Ice Out
Ed Ahern

Winter lets go of the river
with parting waves of snow
and growling goodbyes
as jumbled slabs of ice,
piled shore to shore,
grind stream-grass into confetti
and toted boles of trees
drift on gelid voyages
into flotsam diaspora.

Veiled Water

A. F. Stewart

Reflections in its moving glass,

the ripples of the calm silent sea

a façade above the furtive depths

The soft swoosh of gentle waves

moonlight skims across the surface

Reflections in its moving glass

Siren's call of the lost horizon

and the endless aquatic embrace,

the ripples of the calm silent sea

And isolation sinks in salty liquid

Dive deep from your world

the façade above the furtive depths

Water Women

Matthew Wilson

At night I watch the swirling water

the faces smiling in the waves

that welcome fools as I go forward

to swallow sailors to their graves.

My son was born soft hearted

into those seas he danced free

cursed by a witch so long ago

who swung in a gallows tree.

I was born a coward though

when my boy crept from his bed

devoured by their glinting teeth

turning the shallow water red.

Now I watch the women wave
faces rippling on the eery shore
singing sweetly for me to swim
and in death be afraid no more.

Mother Earth. She grounds us and nurtures life. She consoles, buries, and speaks to what we are made of. Earth encompasses the entirety of sensations from soft fields of tulips to the rocky faces of mountainsides, from fiery spewing volcanoes to silken rivers. Follow along with us to explore this element. From plants that spring from fertile soil to burying things we'd rather leave behind, won't you find out what these poems unearth?

Earth

Kerry E.B. Black

It roils, a quake that splits the ground

Until the truth be found,

Divulging what once was buried

Body left un-ferried

Abandoned by the ferryman

when her love afoul ran.

Demeter: Hollow Earth
Ynes Malakova

Your words are nothing:
A clod of dirt,
Chitin—
A cicada skin
Clinging to the trunk
Of a winter tree.

I should have
Plugged my ears,
Buried my head
And your apology
Under mulch and moss
And, like a mole cricket,
Fiddled proud and strong
Over your
"I'm sorry."

The alveolate promise of

Honey

Cracks—

A cocoon

Under the thin sole of my shoe.

Beaufort 4: All the Elements

Karla Linn Merrifield

Earthwatcher also regards
the sky
before dawn   greeting
Orion before he fades
beneath a glowing blanket
of sun
his surprise this coming day
a corona ringing the waning
October moon
as if he   Great Hunter
had swung his starry
sword round his head
a compass swept through
ice crystals of perfection
signifying his   intentions
to embrace her this hour

to leave her in the light
so she may remember in
waking dreams
his desire --
how he would shield her
if he could
from rising winds
out of the north

While he sleeps in the south
Earthwatcher continues
to regard the heavens
awaiting the storm
due in from Canada.

Crafted from Mountains
JK Allen

Crafted from mountains you sit

    solid as earth.

I watch you from a distance

inhabiting the valley created by you,

    it is your absence.

Craters perch beneath your feet,

    cracked and dry like whispering sand.

You leave an indelible imprint

I can see even from here.

Your voice rumbles

the sounds of rocks tumbling,

a cacophony of boulders

and white teeth.

Your face is painted mud,
red clay and loamy eyes.
You are a peak I will never climb.

Stone Giant
Anna Schoenbach

A giant of green jade,
Sits in his mountain throne.
Full of benevolence, he looks
Onto the world below.

He could help that world,
So the giant thought.
But he stumbled on the slope,
and cracked his nephrite skin.

People saw his kindly heart -
A core of sun-blazed gold,
Coveted, his heart was unearthed,
He was mined away - Put to use - and destroyed.

A hole of cold granite was left,

To collect rainwater on a mountaintop.

No mud could leave it, so it gathered there,

Stinking like hope discarded.

A stray seed falls.

A tiny sprout grows.

Nourished in the stagnant pool,

It mines its green from the mountain again.

Roots conquer stone,

And branches conquer sun,

And shattered hearts grow,

As golden fruits.

Full of benevolence it casts its shade,

To the world below.

The tree thinks "I could help them,

But the world will help itself anyway,

To my shining golden fruit."

Petrichor
Stacy Overby

Cracked and hardened,
hiding a secret,
crazy lines dance away
to a hazy horizon
as clouds gather.

Black smudges
fill the azure sky.

First drops fall
and are sucked down
with nary a trace.

More splatter,
faster and faster
creating soup
stewing on the surface

darker and darker.

It slows to a mist as
a thick scent rises up
revealing itself at last.

Rich, sharp, tang.

Unmistakable smell
reminiscent
of grass and trees
and bugs and 'shrooms.

The smudges thin.

Cerulean vistas return.

But the scent lingers on.

THE CRONE'S ATRIUM
Janet McCann

the atrium's grown wild.
a thorny green dragon now
it grapples with the UPS guy,
parcels get left outside the gate

but I like it, things live there.
the rose bush is 8 feet tall and
there is the ghost of my cat
the dog killed, I believe that now

she has forgiven me. birds rustle
in foliage, it smells of moist earth
and mold and dog pee, who knows what

**lives behind the abandoned
pots under**

the jasmine that has climbed the wall

(from the inside you see only

a green sieve of light) to join the pyracantha

fumbling the eaves, reaching for gutters--

sleeping beauty's castle

a realtor's delight compared to this,

and no one comes to ask about my soul

or sell me Avon and I sit there

on an old metal stool, nuzzled by green.

In the End

Rebecca R. Pierce

Stretching myself across the cool, damp earth,

My fingers dig up fistfuls of dirt.

The ground shudders with thunder. Metal rain

Showers down on men along with the grain.

Dragging myself through the valley floor,

I know I cannot hold on anymore.

The screams that shatter, the bodies that splatter …

What was it all for? Nothing matters.

We had raped the land we sought to hold

Bleeding rubies for a little gold.

That was my thought as I stared at my hand

Dripping crimson to water the land.

A flower touches my cheek as I crawl

Inching like a worm, etching my last scrawl—

A last effort to make my mark, sign my name

On this land that I had tried to claim.

All my struggles had led me to my tomb.

Where the Earth, she claims me like a mother's womb.

Moonlight

Dorothy Tinker

I am the Moonlight, I'm trapped in a stone.

Fingers abrade me, so dark and alone.

You tell me, be pretty. You tell me, be kind.

You tell me the struggle is not worth my time.

But I'm not just beauty, external, for show.

My love and my strength have depths you can't know.

And fight you I will if the purpose is right.

I fight for my people, their stories, my light.

I fight for new business, new books, and new art.

For these are what keep us alive in our hearts.

Yet you say for feelings, this work has no room.

Emotions deceive us, they harm and bring doom.

And so I tried burying my light in your mud,

hoping one day you'd accept who I was.

But I am the Moonlight, not bound by your hate.

My sisters helped pluck me from that deadly fate.

And so I shine forth with my sword and my shield,

and never again to your muck will I yield.

For I am the Moonlight, so dark, wild, and free.

The piece you call moonstone is but part of me.

Progress

Ed Ahern

We were children of Seb the earth god.

Born of soil, arid or fertile,

becoming what we lived within.

But as millennia turned we flinched

away from grounded life,

onto tiers of concrete and asphalt,

transplanted into ersatz

where we were nurtured,

not by earth but by artifice.

We had abandoned Seb

and ate what Shu provided

from the doctored air we lived in

hoping that he did not assume

his aspect as punisher
and flay the pampering skin
of our existence.

Under the Earth
A. F. Stewart

Chocolate loam and mocha dust

burying a lifetime's memories

wrapped in a husband's bones

Death, decay, laid to peaceful rest

ashes to ashes forever, beneath

chocolate loam and mocha dust

Muddy stains on her shoes

impressions in the dirt, footsteps

burying a lifetime's memories

Grains of soil tossed, trickling

Under earth, her broken heart

wrapped in a husband's bones

Duels of Cursed Men

Matthew Wilson

My spurs are music of the dusty street

making mothers tug their children's ear

vanishing from sight on quickly moving feet

when I face the cowboy all locals fear.

They knew he'd sold his spirit to evil

to be the best shot a villain can be

we met beneath the town clock's shadow

to enter combat and secure a victory.

I was quicker on the draw and won the game

here lies the man who killed my wife

I turned away when the clouds darkened

when the devil came for his wicked life.

Now locals whisper my name with fear

no lucky shot could come they say

in time the devil will come and take me

for what I sold him to win the day.

Spirit embodies each element and our ideals. It is all of this and more. Spirit is what we strive for. The following poems reach out for this higher element, exploring the possibilities and even enacting vengeance. Won't you follow along?

Spirit

Kerry E.B. Black

Not to cross the fiery rivers
But point accusing hand
The girl filled with righteous anger
Burst from unsettled land
Her eyes bulged with accusation
Skin fell from bird-thin bones
Until her friend discovered that
He'd never live alone
Flames burned bright blue blame
Skies bowed mourn-filled heads
Winds bore the tale of murder foul
Until he died of shame
And she a spirit on the wind
Spit water from the lake
And gave to pay the passage then
A wedding ring mistake.

She Who Hears the Gods

Ynes Malakova

Oh, Sacred One
Step forth from the mirror
With a sticky coat of foundation
Masking your flaws
And your flashes of eyeliner
Marked with a sniper's precision;
A smudge of shadow
A dusting of blush
Your war paint.

With lips left bare,
You are fire,
Truth-bearer,
A branch of
Yggdrasil
And kindling—

Ashes in the mud
Stamped to soot,
An imprint
Of a sharp-toed boot
Your epitaph.

The breath of the divine
Stirs within,
Brewing with a flood of anguish.
You despair
At the shake of a hand,
A dismissive finger,
Edicts read in flat voices
From stock paper
With cursive letterhead
Calling for your death
Between the lines.

Business as usual.

A bridge between

Two worlds,
You see with eyes
That are not your own,
Speak with wisdom
Beyond yourself,
Smell blood in the fields
Of past and present,
Hear the clash of steel,
Sacred Ones
Reduced to
Locusts and crows.

You alight the world
And are darkness.
Friend of many,
Friend of none.
You are loved and feared,
Woken and sedated,
Beaten and exalted,
Empress and chambermaid.

Goodbye, Glowing Eyes

Anna Schoenbach

Glowing eyes, looking back at me. What do you see?

We are drowning in distance, floating in the void. But can you hear me, my friend? That is my voice -- You know it well.

I am here. Keep looking. Look into the bright screen of the phone, and behold. I cannot touch you, I cannot be there with you, but I can see you;

Your glowing eyes.

Do you see the light differently, my friend? Is it the same for you and me? It doesn't matter.

This light is all we have, and we won't have it for much longer.

Goodbye; Goodbye; my glowing eyes.

Vixen

Dorothy Tinker

I am the Vixen, who plays with her kits.

I tell them my stories of culture and wit.

I tell them be gentle, to make the world kind.

You tell me it's weakness, that surely I'm blind.

Or maybe I'm evil, I've heard that one too.

Your misunderstandings of me are not new.

You see my red hair and no end to my youth.

You call me a liar, unknowing of truth.

But what you don't see, what you fail to digest,

is that I'm a harbor where my kits can rest.

The world can be dark, this I will not refute.

For we are all human, mistakes are our roots.

Yet humans aren't bound by the dark of the night.

You might be surprised that we seek out the light.

As much as we challenge, attack, and defeat,

more often protection we offer to each.

And on to my family and friends I impart

a kind way to handle the world in our hearts.

And so I would ask you to open your minds,

and not to belittle my kits and their kind.

For I am the Vixen, my kits are the world.

I offer my wisdom, then watch them unfurl.

A Universe of Spirit

A. F. Stewart

Golden starlight and moonbeams
beyond the luminosity of grace
There, amid the cosmos, we dream

Rising upward and outward
and we are boundless within
golden starlight and moonbeams

A flicker of infinity's heartbeat
virtuosity connecting, unfolding
beyond the luminosity of grace

Aspiration without limitation
moments of conscious recognition
There, amid the cosmos, we dream

Author Bios

AF Stewart

A steadfast and proud sci-fi and fantasy geek, A. F. Stewart was born and raised in Nova Scotia, Canada and still calls it home. The youngest in a family of seven children, she always had an overly creative mind and an active imagination. She favours the dark and deadly when writing—her genres of choice being fantasy and horror—but she has been known to venture into the light on occasion. As an indie author she's published novels, novellas and story collections, with a few side trips into poetry.

Website:
https://afallonblog.wordpress.com/

Anna Schoenbach

Recently in possession of a new, shiny, Master's Degree in Science Writing from Johns Hopkins University, Anna Schoenbach might be an unlikely person to write poetry... But how else can she capture the overwhelming cacophony of beautiful sensation that is everyday life? Previously published in the poem anthology "Way to my Heart," Anna hopes that she can capture even just a little bit of the awesome power of the natural (and spiritual) world in her writing.

Dorothy Tinker

Dorothy Tinker grew up dreaming of fantastical worlds and creatures, of plots in space, and of strange new cultures. Certain she needed something other than writing to support her through life, she spent her time at the University of Texas at Dallas focusing on math and computer science. Two years after graduating with a BS in applied math, she rediscovered her true passion and rededicated herself to her literary dreams.

Since then, Dorothy has published an ongoing series of young adult fantasy novels, including Peace of Evon, Gift of War, and Lost King. Her short stories have appeared in HWG Press's Riding the Waves and Out of Many, One, Inklings Publishing's Eclectically Cosmic and Eclectically Heroic, and Writespace's In Medias Res.

Dorothy is also the owner of D Tinker Editing and works as copy editor and formatter for Inklings Publishing.

Ed Ahern

Ed Ahern resumed writing after forty odd years in foreign intelligence and international sales. He's had a hundred fifty stories and poems published so far. His collected fairy and folk tales, The Witch Made Me Do It was published by Gypsy Shadow Press. His novella The Witches' Bane was published by World Castle Publishing, and his collected fantasy and horror stories, Capricious Visions was published by Gnome on Pig Press. Ed's currently working on a paranormal/thriller novel tentatively titled The Rule of Chaos. He works the other side of writing at Bewildering Stories, where he sits on the review board and manages a posse of five review editors.

Janet McCann

Journals publishing Janet McCann's work include KANSAS QUARTERLY, PARNASSUS, NIMROD, SOU'WESTER, AMERICA, CHRISTIAN CENTURY, CHRISTIANITY AND LITERATURE, NEW YORK QUARTERLY, TENDRIL, and others. A 1989 NEA Creative Writing Fellowship winner, she taught at Texas A & M University from 1969-2016, is now Professor Emerita. She has co-edited anthologies with David Craig, ODD ANGLES OF HEAVEN (Shaw, 1994), PLACE OF PASSAGE (Story Line, 2000), and POEMS OF FRANCIS AND CLARE (St. Anthony Messenger, 2004). Most recent poetry collection: THE CRONE AT THE CASINO (Lamar University Press, 2014).

JK Allen

JK Allen received her BA in Creative Writing and English from Michigan State University. She wrote her first story when she first learned how to write and hasn't looked back since. Common writing themes that can be found in her work address identity, everyday magic, and the type of strength that can be found in ordinary people. Three of her short stories and several poems are featured in anthologies, and Angelborn is her debut novel coming out this year. She is currently working on the trilogy as well as several shorts, while researching for a new series in the works. Her reading tastes are as varied as the genres she enjoys writing, from Jane Austen to JK Rowling. When she's not writing, you can find her painting, drawing, or lost in another world between the pages of a book. Or on Facebook.

Karla Linn Merrifield

A nine-time Pushcart-Prize nominee and National Park Artist-in-Residence, has had 600+ poems appear in dozens of journals and anthologies. She has 12 books to her credit, the newest of which is Bunchberries, More Poems of Canada, a sequel to Godwit: Poems of Canada (FootHills), which received the Eiseman Award for Poetry. She is assistant editor and poetry book reviewer for The Centrifugal Eye, a member and former board member of Just Poets (Rochester, NY), the Florida State Poetry Society, and The Author's Guild. Visit her woefully outdated, soon-to-be-resurrected blog, Vagabond Poet, at http://karlalinn.blogspot.com. Google her name to learn more; Tweet @LinnMerrifiel.

Kerry EB Black

Kerry E.B. Black resides in a land of bridges and fog-covered rivers where magic happens most every evening. Kerry parents 5 amazing young people and shepherds their menagerie which consists of an excellent service dog named Latte, cats named Poe, Hemingway, and P.D. James, and a super hero Betta fish. Although she enjoys every holiday to the utmost, Kerry strives to make every day a celebration. Please follow the author at
https://kerrylizblack.wordpress.com
www.facebook.com/authorKerryE.B.Black , and Twitter @BlackKerryblick

Matthew Wilson

Matthew Wilson, 33 has been published over 150 times in such places as Horror*Zine, Zimbell House Publishing, Star*Line, Alban Lake and many more. He is currently editing his first novel.

Stacy Overby

Stacy Overby is a regular columnist at ourwriteside.com and her work has been featured in several anthologies, and in issues of OWS Inked, an up and coming literary journal. She is a substance abuse counselor for teenage boys by day and an author by night. Her day job provides inspiration for many of her stories. When not at work or writing, she and her husband are playing with their son, hiking, camping, or involved in other outdoor activities – if it is not too cold. She, along with her social media contacts, can be found at www.thisisnothitchhikersguide.wordpress.com.

Ynes Malakoa

Ynes Malakova holds a deep reverence for beauty found in darkness. She is known for her gothic elegance and intense, lyrical prose. She works incognito in corporate America by day and at night, she curls up with a blanket and a glass of Moscato and writes for intuitive women who experience light, darkness, and the divine as one. Her debut novel, *The Viper Within*, is quickly nearing completion. Ynes has a closet full of sugar skulls, roses, and lace.

Rebecca R Pierce

Rebecca R. Pierce is a published poet and author of short stories. She lives in Atlanta, GA with her husband and daughter, and dotes on one good-for-nothing pug. She is currently working on a paranormal fantasy horror novel The Huntress of Rosefell Hall.

Other Anthologies by Our Write Side

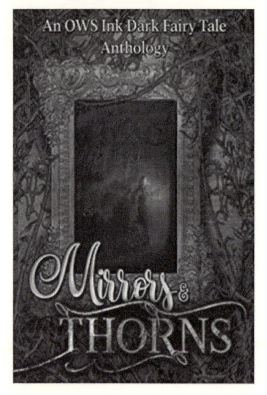

Where the fairy tale ends and the reflection begins... Mirrors & Thorns is a dark fairy tale collection from the twisted pens of J.M. Ames, Kerry E. B. Black, J. K. Allen, C. L. Bledsoe, Lucy Palmer, Stacy Overby, T. S. Dickerson, Edward Ahern, Melanie Noell Bernard, S. L. Scott, Särah Nour, Paul Stansbury, Cassidy Taylor, and J. Lee Strickland

Ambrosia

Whispers to the gods are like honey from a poet's lips. When several poets raise their voices together, it's a sacred feast of memories and dreams. Poetry is divine food for the soul, full of emotion and celestial feeling. Join us in our longing, our pain and passion, heartache, logic and insanity, fear, faith, confusion, hope, unity, solitude, daily life, political strife, and more. From the creative minds of: Eric Keizer, A.L. Mabry, Sam DeLoach, Alyssa Trivett, Mello Sakia, Stacy Overby, Phillip Matthew Roberts, Veronica Falletta and Stephanie Ayers. All royalties go to support the American Foundation for Suicide Prevention.

OWS Ink is a proud supporter of indie authors and publishes a short fiction anthology every year and a poetry anthology as well.

If you would like to submit your own check out

http://ourwriteside.com/submit-annual-anthology/

Custom cover coming soon

Glass & Ashes

Disney's Cinderella, Ella Enchanted, Ever After... all Cinderella stories that are the same, yet very different. They all tell the golden tale of a cellar maid marrying into royalty. But what if...the story changed?

Cinderella created her own destiny?

Someone stole it from her?

Anything else happened but what folklore says it did?

In 2018, we want to celebrate these alternative stories by creating our own versions of Cinderella. Accept the challenge and write your own Cinderella story. Dive deep into the darkest corners of your imagination and weave a tale from 3,500 words to 10,000 words. Offer us a story that would make the Grimm Bros and Hans Christian Anderson want to read it.

Books by Our Write Side

The Dark Archer
Robert Cano-
Coming July 2018

All he wanted was the safety of his princess. What he received was eternal torment.

And now, completely bereft of a soul, a wraith with no ties to humanity, Bene wanted nothing more than death. A release from the twisted existence that had been forced on him.

Trapped between life and nothingness, perhaps if he could reclaim his soul he could find the death he so desperately desired.

Along the way Bene finds rare solace in the company of Feorin. A satyr war hero who had grown tired of the centuries long war with the Fae and finally walked away from it into exile. A lonely life of peace until he met Bene. And Moriactus, a dragon who cares nothing for the world, and only wants to destroy the wraith and all he cherishes.

Dangerous Liaisons

Eighteen months undercover has taken a toll on FBI Agent Sierra Lancaster. So did the shoot out that ended her case and put her and her partner Colton in the hospital. And put a bounty on her head. In an effort to lay low and recover she goes back to her hometown.

But you can never really go back.

Too much has changed, for her and the town she left behind. Her old high school is a front for drug dealers. The love of her life, who betrayed her, is nearly a stranger. Her beloved aunt is ailing, and the truth about her past is coming to light. Sierra has to use all her contacts to find out just what is happening under the façade of the sleepy town she left behind, and who her family really is.

Soul Purge A.L. Mabry-
Coming October 2018

How many times can you watch your love die?

The gift of remembering your past lives and always finding your soul mate is a heavy gift to bear. Especially when you cannot change the outcome.

Be sure to join us at shop.ourwriteside.com to learn more about the many amazing books coming soon!

Made in the USA
Middletown, DE
19 June 2018